No Lex 12-12

WAYNE

GRETZKY

WAYNE GRETZKY

HOCKEY GREAT

Thomas R. Raber

LERNER SPORTS
A DIVISION OF LERNER PUBLISHING GROUP

This book is available in two editions:
Library binding by Lerner Publications Company
Soft cover by First Avenue Editions
Divisions of Lerner Publishing Group
241 First Avenue North
Minneapolis, Minnesota 55401

Website address: www.lernerbooks.com

Website address: www.lernerbooks.com

Library of Congress Cataloging-in-Publication Data

Raber, Thomas R.
    Wayne Gretzky, hockey great / Thomas R. Raber. — Rev. ed.
      p.   cm.
    Includes index.
    Summary: Presents the life and record-setting career of the hockey
player known as "the Great One."
    ISBN 0–8225–3677–3 (alk. paper)
    ISBN 0–8225–9848–5 (alk. paper)
    1. Gretzky, Wayne, 1961– Juvenile literature. 2. Hockey
players—Canada—Biography—Juvenile literature. [1. Gretzky, Wayne,
1961– . 2. Hockey players.] I. Title. II. Title: Wayne Gretzky.
GV848.5.G73R35   1999
796.962'092
[B]—dc21   99–32258

Manufactured in the United States of America
1 2 3 4 5 6 – JR – 05 04 03 02 01 00

Contents

A picture of smoothness, Wayne Gretzky carries the puck down the ice during a Rangers game.

1

The Great One

Rushing down the ice on a **power play** with just 30 seconds left in the second period, number 99 took charge. In his usual style, Wayne Gretzky skated with his helmet low and his body bent at the waist. As always, the Rangers **center** wore his blue jersey tucked in at his right hip but flapping free on his left side.

The play was classic Gretzky. Wayne skated through Pittsburgh **defensemen** and found an open spot on the ice. That spot just happened to be where the puck slid next, as he gently caught a pass from New York's Brian Leetch. Wayne settled the puck with his stick and whipped a pass to teammate

Mathieu Schneider, who was skating at top speed into the **zone.** Schneider faked a shot and sent the puck to Leetch, who scored to tie the game.

Wayne's **assist** on the goal was the 1,963rd of his career, but more important to the thousands of fans watching, it was his last. After 20 seasons, 1,487 games, and 894 goals, the Great One was retiring. This was his last game. Ever.

New York's Madison Square Garden churned with emotion. Thousands of New York Rangers fans had crowded into the arena long before the scheduled start of the last game of the 1998—99 regular season. They carried signs. They cheered. They chanted. Some cried.

The Rangers weren't getting ready for the National Hockey League playoffs. They had been eliminated, for the second straight year, weeks earlier. The visiting Pittsburgh Penguins had made the playoffs. They and their fans were just waiting to see which team they would face. It should have been a meaningless game, before just a few die-hard fans.

Instead, people begged for tickets. Camera crews and reporters flooded the arena. Thousands watched on television. This wasn't just a game to end the season. This game was the last of a record-setting career.

Wayne had announced two days earlier that this game would be his last. "The game doesn't owe me anything," said Wayne, explaining that he didn't want a big ceremony. "The NHL has been outstanding to me. The game of hockey doesn't owe Wayne Gretzky anything. Everything I have, I owe to hockey."

The crowd buzzed with anticipation. Finally, the Garden announcer spoke. He introduced Wayne as the fans thundered their affection for him. Then came Mario Lemieux, who Wayne called "the best player I ever played against," and Mark Messier, who Wayne said was "the best player I ever played with." Wayne's wife, Janet, and his three children—Paulina, Ty, and Trevor—were introduced, along with his mother, Phyllis. Finally, his father, Walter, drove out onto the ice in a shiny black Mercedes, a gift from the team.

"I'm going to miss this game," said Wayne. "I love it. It's a great game. But time does something to you. And it's time."

NHL Commissioner Gary Bettman then announced that no other player in the National Hockey League would ever be allowed to wear the number 99. He said that Wayne had been "a great ambassador" for the sport.

Wayne's family supported him on the day of his retirement. From left, his mother Phyllis, daughter Paulina, son Ty, wife Janet, and son Trevor.

Wayne accomplished more than any other player in the history of hockey. He did it in less time, and he did it with style. He helped his team win four Stanley Cups. He was the Most Valuable Player nine times and the league's leading scorer 10 times. He holds 62 professional hockey records. He played in 18 All-Star Games and was the game's MVP in three of those.

"Wayne Gretzky has done so much for hockey all over the world," said **winger** Teemu Selanne. "The style and the class he has is his own, and nobody can match it off the ice, too. Every player is so thankful and appreciative of what he has done for hockey."

Despite his accomplishments, Wayne is uncomfortable comparing himself to other hockey stars. "In my mind, Gordie Howe is the best player who ever played hockey and the best man who ever played sports," Wayne said. "I just want to be remembered as a guy who always worked hard . . . when I've had an off night I've always forced myself to bounce back."

Following the pregame ceremony, Wayne's final game began. Every time Wayne was on the ice, the crowd held its breath, hoping for more of his on-ice magic. After Wayne's **line** tied the game, neither team scored. The game went into overtime. Quickly, Pittsburgh's star, Jaromir Jagr, ended the drama by poking in the game winner.

Wayne was the first Ranger to congratulate him in the postgame handshake. "I said to a friend that maybe it was fitting that the best young player in the game scored the goal in overtime," Wayne said. "Everybody always talks about passing torches and well, he caught it."

Wayne knows that Jagr and other young players will try to break the records he's set. He remembers that feeling. "The first time I stood on the ice beside [NHL All-Star] Marcel Dionne, I was 18," Wayne says. "I can remember exactly how excited I was. I've seen that same look in younger eyes."

But on April 18, 1999, all eyes were on Wayne Gretzky. After the game ended, Wayne finally gave into his emotions and tears welled up in his eyes. He skated around the rink before collecting Ty and Trevor and his teammates for a group picture. Still, the fans clapped and whistled. He skated around, then got his teammates to skate with him, and finally walked off the ice. But the crowd wouldn't let him go. The fans kept cheering, kept yelling "Gretz-key, Gretz-key." He came back and waved more.

Finally, after waving one last time to the cheering crowd, the greatest hockey player in the history of the game walked off the ice for the last time.

As a youngster, Wayne loved skating and playing hockey from the time he was two. His dad even built him a skating rink in their backyard. Wayne and his dad would practice hockey moves and game situations.

2

Shooting for the Top

Wayne's hockey career began early. He was born on January 26, 1961, in the Canadian town of Brantford, Ontario, which has about 78,000 people and is located about 60 miles southwest of Toronto. Wayne was the first child born to his parents, Walter and Phyllis Gretzky. Later, Wayne was joined by his three brothers—Glen, Keith, and Brent—and his sister, Kim.

Wayne's parents encouraged him in sports from an early age. Even as a two-year-old, Wayne would scoot around the living room with a toy hockey stick and a ball. He would take shots against his grandmother, Mary. She would sit in a chair and be the goaltender.

Wayne's father worked as a teletype repairman. As a young man, Walter Gretzky had played Junior B hockey—a high level of amateur hockey in Canada. When Wayne was four, Walter built a small ice rink in the family's backyard. Wayne's dad even strung up a light so that Wayne could use the rink at night. Wayne's father would water the rink every night with a lawn sprinkler. He would also shave hockey sticks down to Wayne's size.

"I was fortunate to have my dad as my first teacher," Wayne said. "He made the game simple and he made the game fun. He taught me the importance of a lot of hard work."

Wayne practiced hockey almost every day, either in his backyard or at nearby rinks. He and his father would do drills. Sometimes Wayne would skate patterns around cones and tin cans set on the ice. Other times Wayne would jump over sticks placed on the ice as he received passes from his father. In this way, the Gretzkys tried to imitate the obstacles Wayne would face in game situations. Often Wayne shot at targets his father had made. The targets got smaller as Wayne got better.

When Wayne was six, he joined his first organized hockey team. The rest of his teammates were 10 years old. As Wayne grew, he continued to play with boys older than he was. He was almost always the youngest and smallest player on his teams, but he played as if he were much older. At age eight, he scored 104 goals in 40 games. At age nine, he had 196 goals and 316 **points** in 76 games. The next year, Wayne scored 378 goals in 82 games.

Young Wayne became famous throughout Canada.

Sometimes Wayne's dad would throw a puck into a corner of the rink and urge Wayne to chase it. Wayne would follow the puck. His dad would yell, "Skate to where the puck's going to be, not to where it has been. Anticipate. Anticipate."

Wayne practiced hard, but playing hockey was fun for him. No one needed to push him. "Wayne motivated himself," his dad once said. But it's important to remember that much of Wayne's talent was an inborn gift.

Wayne's father went to all of Wayne's games. As they drove home, Wayne and his dad would discuss the game. They would review where Wayne or his teammates had been during a certain play and where, perhaps, they should have been.

Hockey is the most popular sport in Canada, and news of the young superstar spread fast. By the time Wayne was 10, opposing teams began assigning specific players to **check** him. The next year, Wayne played 9 games during a weekend tournament and scored 50 goals. Newspaper and television reporters wanted to interview Wayne. Some people wanted his autograph. It wasn't long before crowds at games became so large that Wayne sometimes needed a police escort just to get in and out of the arena.

When he was 11 years old, Wayne got a chance to meet his idol, Gordie Howe, at a sports banquet in Brantford. Howe played for the Detroit Red Wings and had become hockey's all-time leading scorer in 1960. The pro star offered Wayne some advice the young player never forgot. "Make sure you keep practicing that backhand," Howe told Wayne.

The Gretzky children were all involved in sports. Wayne's sister, Kim, ran track. Glen played hockey when he was young. Keith became a minor league hockey player. Wayne ran track and played hockey, lacrosse, and baseball. Brent, the youngest Gretzky, went on to play professional hockey, too.

By the time Wayne was a teenager, he had his sights set on a career in hockey. But two obstacles stood in his way. First, he was not very big. At the time, pro teams were especially interested in big, strong players. Wayne was neither big nor strong. Wayne's father advised him not to count on a pro career.

Second, Wayne was unhappy. He should have been enjoying himself and his hockey talent. But he felt pressure, mainly from the parents of some of his teammates and opponents. They said Wayne was getting too much playing time. They said Wayne wanted all the glory for himself.

Gordie Howe playfully tugs at Wayne when the two met at a sports banquet. Howe played for the Detroit Red Wings and set many of the records Wayne later broke. Wayne says Howe is the greatest hockey player ever.

Spectators sometimes jeered Wayne during games and hassled him off the ice. People even called the Gretzkys' home to make rude comments. "The biggest disease in the world is jealousy," Wayne says. "If someone sees their child isn't doing as well as the next child, they take it out on the [successful] child. That's unfortunate."

One solution for Wayne was to leave home. He could live in another city. He could go to school and play hockey somewhere else. The idea sounded strange at first. Wayne's parents were against the move. But eventually the Gretzkys formed a plan.

Wayne moved to Toronto to live with family friends. He would go to school there and play Junior B hockey. Wayne was 14 years old. Some of the other Junior B players were 20!

"I wasn't enjoying the atmosphere in Brantford, the peer pressure," Wayne says. "It was so difficult for me just to go to school, such a big thing to knock off Gretzky. A lot of people thought I moved away from home to be a hockey player, but that's not why. I moved away to just try to escape all the pressures parents place on kids."

Wayne played Junior B hockey in Toronto for two years. Wayne called his family every night, and the

Gretzkys drove to see as many of Wayne's games as they could.

At first, Wayne was excited about the move. But soon he felt lonely and sad.

"Lying in bed the first night in Toronto, I thought it was the greatest thing in the world," Wayne says. "Three days later it came to me, 'Oh no, what am I doing here?' I was homesick for a year."

Wayne had to get used to living in a new place. He had to change schools a few times, and he had to do some schoolwork by mail. The experience was difficult, but it taught him independence.

Wayne was popular as a teenager. He could have had many dates. But he seldom asked anyone out, and he never saw anyone steadily. He didn't drink, smoke, or even drive. Wayne focused on hockey.

"My father always told me to get what I wanted most and the rest would follow," Wayne said. What Wayne wanted most was a hockey career.

By the time he was 17, Wayne began playing Junior A hockey for the Sault Sainte Marie Greyhounds. Until then, Wayne had always worn number 9 on his jersey in honor of Gordie Howe, who also wore that number. But the number 9 was already taken on Wayne's new team. So Wayne switched to number 99.

Sault Sainte Marie, Ontario, is 500 miles from Brantford. Again Wayne changed schools and moved in with family friends. His family was rarely able to travel to see his games. But by this time, it was clear that Wayne's hockey career would be taking him even farther away from home.

After a season of Junior A hockey, Wayne was voted the league rookie of the year and named its most sportsmanlike player. Then, just three years after leaving home, Wayne signed a professional contract with the Indianapolis Racers of the World Hockey Association (WHA). It was 1978. Wayne was just 17.

But the Racers, like many teams in the WHA, were having money problems. Eight games into the 1978–79 season, Wayne and two other players were traded to the Edmonton Oilers of Alberta, Canada.

With the Oilers, Wayne became the WHA's rookie of the year. But the WHA folded the next season. The National Hockey League took in the Edmonton Oilers and three other WHA teams for the 1979–80 season.

Wayne's dream had come true. He was playing in the National Hockey League. But it was only the beginning for the Great One.

Walter Gretzky, Wayne's dad, looks on as Wayne signs a contract with the Edmonton Oilers of the World Hockey Association. Wayne was just 18 when he was traded to the Oilers.

3

The Right Angles

When Wayne burst into the National Hockey League at age 19, he was one of the youngest players in the league. Wayne was also small for the NHL, at 6 feet and about 170 pounds. But those challenges were nothing new for Wayne.

In the 1979–80 season, his first in the NHL, Wayne won the Hart Trophy as the league's Most Valuable Player. He also won the league's Lady Byng Trophy as the player with the most sportsmanship. Wayne was the youngest player in history to win an NHL trophy. He was also the youngest ever to be named to the NHL All-Star team. Wayne compiled 137 points and finished third in the league scoring race.

But Wayne was just getting started. The next season, 1980—81, Wayne set a record for points in a season—164—better than the previous all-time mark of 152 set by Phil Esposito when he skated for the Boston Bruins.

That season, Wayne also broke Bobby Orr's record for assists in a season. Orr had 102. Wayne had 109. Orr had been a stick-handling and skating whiz for the Boston Bruins in the 1970s. After watching Wayne, Orr was quick to praise Wayne's skill. "He passes far better than anybody I've ever seen and he thinks so far ahead," said Orr.

The next year, Wayne recorded 212 points with 92 goals. He had broken Phil Esposito's record for most goals in a season by 16! In his first 39 games, Wayne scored 50 goals. That shattered Maurice "The Rocket" Richard's mark of 50 goals in 50 games, which had stood since 1945 and had been equaled only once.

Richard had been a top shooter for the Montreal Canadiens during the 1940s and 1950s. Wayne's talent amazed Richard. "I've seen some good skaters, but they were never like Gretzky," he said. "There's no way anyone will stop him from being the greatest star in hockey."

Wayne was just 21. But the marks he was setting were so far beyond the previous records that they were hard to understand. Wayne was rewriting the hockey record books and changing the game.

"Hockey needed a shot in the arm when he came along," said Hall of Famer Bobby Hull, who was a top scorer for the Chicago Blackhawks during the 1960s. "It needed a champion. People are again relating to hockey as a game of skill, because that's the way Wayne plays."

Some fans had thought of hockey as merely a bruising game—until Wayne came along. Wayne was not a rough-and-tough player. He was not big, but a rough style wouldn't have suited him anyway.

Wayne's game was marked by quickness, agility, and spirit. He wasn't a very graceful skater, and his skating speed was about average. But he had excellent balance, an extremely accurate shot, and uncanny puck-handling skills.

Many experts talk about Wayne's "hockey sense." He seemed to anticipate where the puck was headed next. He saw two or three plays ahead in the game and then chose the best course of action. "Wayne is a perfectionist who is blessed with the gift of total concentration," said Gordie Howe.

Most pro players look at the individuals on the ice, but Wayne looked at situations. He thought of all of his teammates—not just the one or two players who were in his sight—as part of the play. He thought about the entire rink, not just the ice that was in front of him.

Wayne's vision was valuable even when he did not have the puck. He knew how to play without the puck and how to get open. He saw openings, and he created them.

"People talk about skating, puck handling, and shooting," Wayne said, "but the whole sport is angles and caroms [rebounds], forgetting the straight direction the puck is going, calculating where it will be diverted, factoring in all the interruptions. Basically my whole game is angles."

Much of Wayne's ability came from his natural talent. No amount of practice could turn a lesser athlete into another Wayne Gretzky. But Wayne practiced tirelessly to make the most of his gifts.

"I'm the first to admit I've been God blessed," Wayne said, "but I also know I've worked hard for everything I got."

Like most champions, Wayne had the ability to rise to an occasion. He was at his best when the

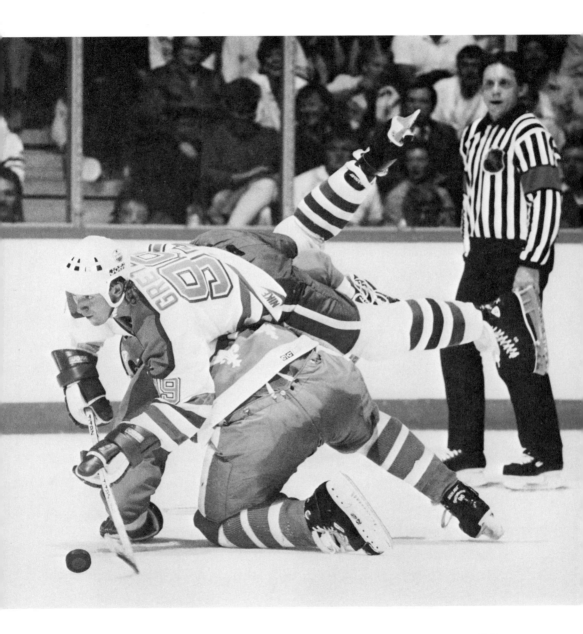

pressure was greatest. Wayne had a knack for making his teammates play better, too. He set them up with his good passes, but he also inspired them.

"You see him working so hard every second. This is the best player in the world, so how can you not try to work that hard?" said winger Luc Robitaille.

Wayne used his balance and anticipation to avoid collisions. Opponents may have connected with Wayne, but he was often able to lean away from the blow and soften the impact.

"There isn't a center in the league I can outmuscle," Wayne admitted. "I played a lot of lacrosse, and that taught me how to roll with checks, slip away from them. . . . People say players in the NHL won't hit me. They all want to hit me. But they have to catch me first!"

Wayne had weaknesses, too. Some said Wayne was not a good player on defense. But even Wayne's presence on the ice was a type of defense. When Wayne was playing, the opposition had to think about stopping him. "If I've got it [the puck], they can't score," Wayne said. And even when Wayne didn't have the puck, opponents had to keep an eye on him, sometimes leaving Wayne's teammates open in the process.

By 1982, nothing Wayne accomplished came as a surprise. In fact, many of the records Wayne broke were his own. The 200-point plateau was once unimaginable in hockey, but Wayne scored more than 200 points in each of four seasons between 1981 and 1986.

Wayne enjoyed his records, but what he wanted most was for his team to win. That did not happen. In the 1982—83 playoffs, the New York Islanders shut down Wayne. He did not score a goal in the Islanders—Oilers series. The Islanders swept the Oilers four games, and went on to win their fourth consecutive Stanley Cup.

The Edmonton fans were the first to call Wayne "the Great One." Would they ever get to see hockey's greatest player hold high the Stanley Cup?

Wayne skates off after scoring one of his 894 goals.

4

Great Seasons

Wayne began the 1983—84 season more dedicated and determined than ever. As a result, he reeled off an amazing scoring streak. From October 5, 1983, to January 28, 1984, Wayne scored at least one point in 51 straight games. That's a record that is likely to stand for a long, long time.

"This may have been one of the harder records to break," Wayne said. "When you score 90 goals or break the record for points, you can do that over 80 games. But the streak itself is pressure every night to be at your best, be consistent game in and game out."

But best of all, Wayne finished the year on a winning streak. Edmonton won its first Stanley Cup!

Wayne also was the NHL's Most Valuable Player for the fifth time, and he compiled 205 points.

"I enjoy hockey even more now that I can say I'm a champion," Wayne said. "To be champion changes everything, just the way you feel about coming to the rink. Many a time I've stared and stared at the Stanley Cup."

With Wayne as captain, the Oilers became not only one of the most successful teams in the league but also one of the most exciting. Playing with other stars, such as Jari Kurri, Mark Messier, Kevin Lowe, and Paul Coffey, Wayne continued to improve.

Wayne was becoming more mature on the ice. He had once had a reputation for whining to the officials. He would sometimes take "dives" on the ice. If an opponent collided with him, Wayne might exaggerate his fall. He might lie on the ice just a bit too long before getting up. Some critics and players called him a "crybaby." Wayne was hoping the official would call a penalty against the other player.

But no more. By 1984, Wayne had changed his ways. He didn't like his reputation as a complainer. "The big thing with me is that I play emotionally," Wayne said. "I used to let the emotion run away with me. If I got fouled, I'd blame the ref or the other player. Now my attitude is, if the ref calls it, fine; if not, I'm not going to change his mind." With his new attitude, Wayne bettered his record for assists with 135 in 1984–85, and the Oilers won their second straight Stanley Cup.

In 1985–86, Wayne enjoyed his finest scoring season. He scored 52 goals and had 163 assists, giving him 215 points—marks that still stand as Wayne's best and all of hockey's best for a season. But the Calgary Flames defeated the Oilers in the quarterfinals of the Stanley Cup playoffs. In the deciding game, Steve Smith, a rookie defenseman, accidentally knocked the puck into his own net. The Flames won the game by a single goal. Smith's error had cost the defending champion Oilers a chance at their third straight postseason championship.

A year later, in the 1986–87 season, Wayne led the league in scoring during the regular season (183 points) and in the playoffs (34). He led the Oilers back into the playoffs. When Edmonton beat the Philadelphia Flyers in seven games for the Cup, Wayne showed why he was the team captain.

Wayne accepted the Stanley Cup trophy at **center ice** and searched for Steve Smith. He wanted Smith to be the first Oiler teammate to hold the Cup high.

A whole year had gone by since Smith's mistake and Wayne knew how much the victory meant to the young player.

That September, Wayne served as captain of Team Canada, a hockey team that represented Canada against five other countries in the Canada Cup tournament. Wayne led all tournament players in points with 3 goals and 18 assists in 9 games. Team Canada won the event by defeating the Soviet Union. Many spectators rated Canada's three playoff games against the Soviets to be some of the most exciting hockey ever played. The score of all three games was 6–5, and the first two games went into overtime.

Wayne's playmaking was decisive in the final game. With less than a minute and a half left in the game, Wayne sent a perfect pass to teammate Mario Lemieux, who took Wayne's pass and shot home the winning goal.

"The Canada Cup was my greatest thrill," Wayne said. "I said to the boys in the dressing room, 'Every kid in Canada would love to be playing right now and doing what we're doing,' and it's true."

Wayne returned to his NHL duties for the 1987–88 season. The pressure of being the most famous person in Canada seemed to be wearing him down.

Ever since he was a young boy, Wayne had been in the national spotlight. For years he had handled the attention pretty well, but he was getting tired. He began to talk about retiring. He was only 26, but he had been playing hockey a long time. Some fans whispered that Wayne was slowing down.

On December 30, 1987, Wayne was knocked into a goal post. He sprained ligaments in his left knee. The injury kept him out of 13 games. Later in the season, a stick caught him in the eye and sidelined him for three more games.

During Wayne's first absence, Mario Lemieux, the big center from Pittsburgh, took over the scoring lead. Wayne never could catch him. Wayne's totals that season would have been great for any other player, but 40 goals were a career low for him. His 149 points marked his lowest output since he had recorded 137 as a rookie.

Lemieux, not Wayne, was the star of the 1987–88 season. Lemieux won the Hart Trophy for the Most Valuable Player, which Wayne had owned for eight straight seasons. Lemieux also won the scoring title that Wayne had held for seven years.

Still, Wayne led the league in assists for the ninth straight season and led the Oilers to yet another

Stanley Cup championship. He set an NHL record for most assists in the playoffs, 31 in 19 games, and most in the series final, with 10. He also earned his second Conn Smythe Trophy as the best player in the playoffs. Wayne's teammate Mark Messier said after the playoffs, "He played like he never has before."

Mark Messier, second from the left, and Wayne celebrate the Oilers' fourth Stanley Cup.

5

Traded

Winning his fourth Stanley Cup wasn't all Wayne had to celebrate in 1988. On the afternoon of July 16, 1988, he married Janet Jones in Edmonton. Wayne and Janet had announced their engagement in January 1988. Canada had six months to anticipate the event, which was probably the most publicized wedding in Canadian history. There were 600 guests at the wedding, and a large crowd of well-wishers gathered for blocks around the church.

Wayne had met Janet on the set of an American television show called *Dance Fever*. Janet was a regular dancer on the show, and Wayne appeared one time as a celebrity judge. Wayne and Janet share a love of sports. Janet swims, dives, and plays softball. She is an actor, so she knows the demands of performing in public.

"She's a great lady who understands the pressures that I'm under," Wayne said. "Obviously, being in pressure situations herself, she can relate to it."

On August 9, 1988, less than a month after the wedding, Wayne found himself in the news again. The Great One had been traded! The Oilers had sent Wayne and two other players to the Los Angeles Kings for two players, three future first-round draft choices, and $15 million.

At a press conference in Edmonton, Wayne was in tears. He choked out a good-bye to the people of Edmonton. Then he flew to Los Angeles.

Hockey fans were shocked. Wayne was a national hero in Canada. Just 24 days earlier, the whole country had gone crazy over his wedding. When he was traded, Canadians felt they were losing Wayne to the United States.

Some Oiler fans made up rude signs and sayings about Oilers owner Peter Pocklington, the man who traded Wayne. Oiler defenseman Kevin Lowe said what was on many fans' minds: "How do you replace Wayne Gretzky?"

Wayne was as stunned as anyone.

"At that point, I felt like everyone else," Wayne said later. "I couldn't believe it was happening. It wasn't as if we had just lost. We had just won the Stanley Cup for the fourth time in five years. I'd had, arguably, my best playoff ever and all of a sudden, I'm traded."

News of the trade was surrounded by rumors. Wayne's contract was due to expire in 1992, and he would be free to play for another team. If the Oilers waited until then, they would lose their star player and get nothing in return.

Some people said Wayne had asked the Oilers to trade him. Others thought that Pocklington, hoping to avoid a trade, had offered to give Wayne a new contract. But Wayne did not want to give up the chance to become a free agent and see what other teams would offer to pay him. Some people thought Wayne was greedy not to agree to sign with the Oilers again. Others thought he was smart to find out what he was worth to other teams.

Some people blamed the trade on Janet Gretzky. Some thought she wanted Wayne traded to Los Angeles so she could be closer to her acting career in Hollywood. Wayne said his wife was not behind the trade.

Wayne soon saw a good side to being traded. Southern California is filled with famous people. Wayne would blend in. He wouldn't stand alone as one big star in Los Angeles. "I'm only in the sports section here," Wayne said of Los Angeles.

Wayne was also concerned for his family's privacy. His daughter, Paulina, was born in 1988. "People won't know who our kids are," Wayne said. "That wouldn't have been possible in Canada. Let's face it. The child would be under a microscope living in Canada. In L. A., she is just another child in the crowd. Everybody always treated us first-class there [in Edmonton], but we had absolutely no privacy. . . . You always felt like you were on display."

In Los Angeles, Wayne quickly felt at home. In the season opener against the Detroit Red Wings, Wayne scored on the first shot he took. He added three assists in the game and helped the Kings win, 8—2. Wayne showed he was the same player he'd always been.

The Kings drew a sellout crowd for the home opener of 1988. The team got off to a 4—0 start, the best in its history. Average attendance at Kings games increased by more than 3,200 people per game. Many were new fans, coming to watch Wayne.

Before Wayne joined the Kings, they had rarely been successful. But with Wayne, they posted the fourth best record in the league: 42—31—7 in the regular season. They finished second in their division, ahead of the Oilers. The Kings beat the defending champion Oilers in the first round of the playoffs. The Kings were later eliminated in the 1988—89 division finals.

Early in the next season, Wayne and the Kings had another important encounter with the Oilers. On October 15, 1989, a sellout crowd of 17,503 fans jammed into the Northlands Coliseum in Edmonton to watch the game between the Oilers and the Kings. Wayne had asked his wife, his father, and Gordie Howe to be there, also.

Everyone was expecting Wayne to make history that night. Howe, who had played for the Detroit Red Wings, was hockey's leading scorer with 801 goals and 1,049 assists for 1,850 points. He had surpassed the Montreal Canadiens' great Maurice "Rocket" Richard on January 16, 1960. Howe took the lead with 965 points and added another 885 to his grand total before retiring in the 1970s after playing 1,767 games in 26 seasons. Howe's hold on the record had stood for almost 30 years.

After Wayne joined the NHL in 1979, he began racking up points faster than any other player in the history of pro hockey. By the start of the 1989–90 season, Wayne was just 13 points behind Howe.

Edmonton fans wanted to see Wayne break Howe's record. Wayne was a Los Angeles King, but he had once played for the Edmonton Oilers. And, to the people of Canada, he was still a hero.

Late in the game, the Kings trailed the Oilers, 4–3, and Wayne had not scored. Like many teams, the Oilers had assigned some of their toughest defensive players to cover Wayne. They had hoped to rough up Wayne and slow him down. The strategy had worked.

Then, with less than a minute left, Wayne circled behind the Oilers' net. He set himself close to the left of the goal and waited. The puck came his way. It glanced off another player and skipped across the front of the net to Wayne's stick. With 53 seconds remaining, Wayne flipped the puck past the Oilers goaltender and into the net.

Wayne turned and danced toward his teammates. All of the Kings left the bench to greet him. With his game-tying goal, Wayne had become the all-time leading scorer in the history of professional hockey!

Wayne and Gordie Howe show off their record-setting pucks, which are kept in the Hockey Hall of Fame.

This was the 641st goal of Wayne's career. When combined with his 1,210 assists, he had 1,851 career points. It had taken Wayne only 780 games and just more than 10 seasons to break Howe's record.

"I actually think Wayne felt a little bit bad about breaking the record," Howe said. "That's the kind of kid he is. He wanted to do it and he had to do it. He couldn't go the rest of the season without any points. But he didn't want to see me hurt by it all."

The Edmonton fans gave Wayne a three-minute standing ovation. A representative from the National Hockey League Hall of Fame collected the puck and stick Wayne used for the record. He picked up Wayne's jersey after the game. Wayne scored another goal that night to give the Kings a 5–4 victory over Edmonton.

Wayne was back up to speed. Once again, he led the league in scoring. But the Kings were still a mediocre team. They placed fourth in the Smythe Division. In the 1990 division semifinals, the Kings beat Calgary in six games. But Edmonton then swept the Kings 4–0 in the division finals. "As ecstatic as we were last year after beating Edmonton [in the division semifinals], I'm disappointed," Wayne said at the season's end. "I hate losing."

On October 23, 1990, Wayne became the first player to score 2,000 points. Still, the highlight of the year for Wayne was the birth of his son, Ty, in 1990. Wayne also led the league with 164 points for the season. The Kings ended the 1990—91 season with a respectable 46—24—10 record, yet lost to Edmonton in the second round of the division playoffs.

At the beginning of the 1991—92 season, Wayne was suffering from a serious back injury. Janet and Wayne's second son, Trevor, was born in 1992. Wayne also took time off to visit his father, who was seriously ill. Eventually, his father began to recover. Wayne's back healed and he earned a league-leading 90 assists. The Kings finished the season at 35—31—14. But in the division semifinals, they lost to Edmonton again.

Another back injury caused Wayne to miss the first half of the 1992—93 season. When he returned, the Kings shifted into high gear. They took on Montreal in the Stanley Cup finals. The Kings won the first game of the series but dropped the next four and lost the series. Despite the Kings' second-place finish, Wayne had an incredible playoff series. With 15 goals, 25 assists, and 40 points, he was the leading scorer in the playoffs.

One of Wayne's biggest records was set on March 23, 1994. He scored his 802nd goal, breaking Howe's long-standing record to become the NHL's all-time leading goal-scorer. Wayne again led the league in points and assists. The Kings finished the 1993—94 season at fifth in their division.

Los Angeles went from fifth to fourth place in the division in 1994—95, but Wayne had his worst season ever. For the first time in his 17-year NHL career, he did not lead the league in goals, assists, or points. He finished the season with 48 points.

Wayne tried to direct attention away from himself, but he was under the spotlight again the following season. "I don't think anybody needs to get into a war of words," Wayne said. "I never argue with people. You can't win. I just walk away from it. If I order a steak medium rare and it comes back well done, I eat it. Life's too short. I've got more important things in life to worry about."

The 1995—96 season put those words to the test. Wayne was tired of being seen as the Kings' only solid player. He asked the management to build a winning team or trade him. In the middle of the season, the Kings traded him. On February 27, 1996, the Great One went to the St. Louis Blues.

Brett Hull and Wayne were teammates in St. Louis.

At Home in New York

At first, Wayne was happy to be in St. Louis. The Blues were a good team, and he got a chance to play on his friend Brett Hull's line. Just as he had with the Kings, Wayne scored a goal in his first game with the Blues. But as the season wore on, the Blues coaches thought Wayne should be doing more. They weren't satisfied with his 21 points in 18 games, so they did not sign him to a new contract.

Wayne made a lot of money playing hockey— more than $5 million a year, including his earnings from commercial endorsements. But he once said, "I'd rather be broke and have friends than be rich and not have friends. That's my philosophy, because with friends you can go a long way. With money, you can become awfully lonely. Hockey will always be number two to my family," Wayne said. "And to me, friends are more important than business."

As a superstar, Wayne could have gone wherever he wanted, and some teams had offered him more than the New York Rangers did. But he said he decided to go to New York because he would be able to play with his old friend and teammate, Mark Messier.

After joining the Rangers on July 21, 1996, Wayne said, "For Wayne Gretzky, the hardest thing now is that I'm being compared to myself." In the middle of the 1996–97 season, some fans said Wayne had lost his magic when he went 21 games without a goal. But on February 21, 1997, he scored his 900th career goal—his 854th in the NHL—and broke the slump.

After he helped the Rangers into the playoffs, his magic reappeared. Wayne scored the ninth playoff **hat trick** of his career in the quarterfinals, and the 10th in the semifinals. The New Jersey Devils beat the Rangers in the semifinals.

After the 1996–97 season, Pittsburgh star Mario Lemieux retired because of health problems. Lemieux had challenged Wayne's records and had a better goals-per-game average than Wayne.

Mark Messier and Wayne played together in New York.

The two had been friendly rivals. "If he hadn't gone through all the back problems and cancer," Wayne said, "he might have been the guy who . . . shattered all my records."

Wayne's dream of winning another Stanley Cup with Messier as his teammate was also dashed after his first season in New York. The Rangers did not come to terms with Messier and he left to play for the Vancouver Canucks.

Even though Wayne would not be sharing a Cup victory with Messier, he wanted another chance at a championship. After nearly two decades in the NHL, Wayne held most of the league's major scoring records. He was slowing down, but he could still anticipate the puck's movement and set up plays with uncanny skill.

The 1997–98 season did not go well for Wayne. Wayne, along with many other NHL players, took a break in the middle of the season to play in the Olympic Games. The Canadian team had been expected to win the gold medal but finished third. Wayne did not score a goal in any of the team's six games, but he had four assists. He finished the NHL season with 23 goals and 90 points, but the Rangers did not make the playoffs.

Wayne struggled for the first part of the 1998–99 season, playing despite an injured disk in his neck. By the middle of his 20th NHL season, he had regained his form. For the 18th time in his career, he was named to play in the All-Star Game. He scored a goal—his 13th All-Star Game goal—and had two assists. After his dazzling display, he was named the game's MVP, which was the third time he had won that honor.

Two nights later, on his 38th birthday, Wayne had three assists to lead the Rangers to a 4—1 victory over the Washington Capitals. "It was something that maybe gave me a little bit of an extra jump start," said Wayne. "It was a fun weekend."

He shoots. He scores! Wayne scores another goal at the 1999 All-Star Game.

The rest of the season wasn't so much fun. Wayne's neck continued to bother him and the Rangers continued to lose. Finally, after he had played in 222 consecutive games for New York, Wayne sat out for about a month and missed 12 games.

Wayne might have stayed out longer with the injury but the Rangers were struggling to make the playoffs. He rejoined the team in mid-March. "I mostly tried to encourage everybody and stay out of the way," said Wayne after the Rangers lost the game he returned for.

A week later, Wayne kept his team's dwindling playoff hopes alive by scoring the game-winning goal with just more than two minutes left in a game with the Islanders. The goal also set another record for Wayne. It was his 1,072 career professional goal (WHA and NHL combined) and put him one past Gordie Howe's mark.

"It was a nice goal at a nice time," said Wayne. "The most important thing about it was that it was such a big goal. I'm just happy it was a goal that had value to the team. At a time we desperately needed a win, I was obviously ecstatic that it went in."

It was Wayne's last goal. He finished his last season with nine goals and 53 assists. The Rangers did not make the playoffs.

Wayne knows that there is more to the world than hockey sticks and pucks. "Lots of times I wished I'd gone to university," Wayne says. "But I've lived a great life, been to lots of places, and I owe it all to hockey. You can't have it all."

Since Wayne retired, he has more time for his other sports, namely golf, tennis, and softball. He also spends time working for charity. Years ago, he met and was inspired by a blind wrestler from northern Ontario. Wayne founded an annual softball tournament in Brantford that benefits the Canadian National Institute for the Blind.

Wayne has always been willing to sign autographs and meet fans. Although he is shy, Wayne has been, and probably always will be, an ambassador for the sport of hockey.

"A lot of athletes forget who they are and how they got where they are," Wayne said. "My main focus is hockey, but I believe you have to give something back to the game. I owe everything I have to hockey. It's given me . . . a chance to see the world, to meet some great people. I get paid a lot of money for something that I love to do. And when you think you're bigger than your sport, you're in trouble."

Statistics

Ontario Major Junior Hockey League

Season	Team	Regular Season				Playoffs			
		Games	Goals	Assists	Points	Games	Goals	Assists	Points
1976–77	Peterborough	3	0	3	3	—	—	—	—
1977–78	Sault Ste. Marie	64	70	112	182	13	6	20	26
	Totals	67	70	115	185	13	6	20	26

World Hockey Association

Season	Team	Regular Season				Playoffs			
		Games	Goals	Assists	Points	Games	Goals	Assists	Points
1978–79	Indianapolis	8	3	3	6	—	—	—	—
	Edmonton	72	43	61	104	13	10	10	20
	Totals	80	46	64	110	13	10	10	20

Wayne began his professional career in Indianapolis in 1978.

National Hockey League

Season	Team	Regular Season				Playoffs			
		Games	Goals	Assists	Points	Games	Goals	Assists	Points
1979–80	Edmonton	79	51	86	137	3	2	1	3
1980–81	Edmonton	80	55	109	164	9	7	14	21
1981–82	Edmonton	80	92	120	212	5	5	7	12
1982–83	Edmonton	80	71	125	196	16	12	26	38
1983–84	Edmonton	74	87	118	205	19	13	22	35
1984–85	Edmonton	80	73	135	208	18	17	30	47
1985–86	Edmonton	80	52	163	215	10	8	11	19
1986–87	Edmonton	79	62	121	183	21	5	29	34
1987–88	Edmonton	64	40	109	149	19	12	31	43
1988–89	Los Angeles	78	54	114	168	11	5	17	22
1989–90	Los Angeles	73	40	102	142	7	3	7	10
1990–91	Los Angeles	78	41	122	163	12	4	11	15
1991–92	Los Angeles	74	31	90	121	6	2	5	7
1992–93	Los Angeles	45	16	49	65	24	15	25	40
1993–94	Los Angeles	81	38	92	130	—	—	—	—
1994–95	Los Angeles	48	11	37	48	—	—	—	—
1995–96	Los Angeles	62	15	66	81	—	—	—	—
	St. Louis	18	8	13	21	13	2	14	16
1996–97	N.Y. Rangers	82	25	72	97	15	10	10	20
1997–98	N.Y. Rangers	82	23	67	90	—	—	—	—
1998–99	N.Y. Rangers	70	9	53	62	—	—	—	—
	Totals	1,487	894	1,963	2,857	208	122	260	382

Highlights

- Most goals in a season, 92 in 1981–82
- Most assists in a season, 163 in 1985–86
- Most consecutive games scoring a point, 51, from Oct. 5, 1983 to Jan. 28, 1984
- Most career NHL regular-season points, 2,857
- Most NHL scoring titles, 10
- Most seasons with 100 or more points, 15
- Most times named league Most Valuable Player, 9
- Member of four Stanley Cup championship teams, 1984, 1985, 1987, 1988

NHL Records Held or Shared by Wayne Gretzky

Wayne holds or shares 61 records listed in the NHL Official Guide and Record Book: 40 for the regular season, 15 for the Stanley Cup playoffs and six for the All-Star Game. In addition, he holds the unofficial record for the most goals scored in the World Hockey Association and NHL, 1,702.

Regular-Season Records (40)

- MOST GOALS: 894 (1,485 games)
- MOST GOALS, INCLUDING PLAYOFFS: 1,016 — 894 regular season and 122 playoff
- MOST GOALS, ONE SEASON: 92—1981–82, 80-game schedule
- MOST GOALS, ONE SEASON, INCLUDING PLAYOFFS: 100—1983–84, 87 goals in 74 regular season games and 13 goals in 19 playoff games.
- MOST GOALS, 50 GAMES FROM START OF SEASON: 61—1981–82 (Oct. 7, 1981 to Jan. 22, 1982, 80-game schedule); 1983–84 (Oct. 5, 1983 to Jan. 25, 1984, 80-game schedule)
- MOST GOALS, ONE PERIOD: 4—(Tied with 10 other players) Feb. 18, 1981, at Edmonton, third period (Edmonton 9, St. Louis 2)
- MOST ASSISTS: 1,962 (1,485 games)
- MOST ASSISTS, INCLUDING PLAYOFFS: 2,222—1,962 regular season and 260 playoff
- MOST ASSISTS, ONE SEASON: 163 - 1985-86, 80-game schedule
- MOST ASSISTS, ONE SEASON, INCLUDING PLAYOFFS: 174—1985-86, 163 assists in 80 regular-season games and 11 assists in 10 playoff games
- MOST ASSISTS, ONE GAME: 7—(tied with Billy Taylor) done three times— Feb. 15, 1980 at Edmonton (Edmonton 8, Washington 2); Dec. 11, 1985 at Chicago (Edmonton 12, Chicago 9); Feb. 14, 1986 at Edmonton (Edmonton 8, Quebec 2)
- MOST ASSISTS, ONE ROAD GAME: 7 (tied with Billy Taylor)—Dec. 11, 1985 at Chicago (Edmonton 12, Chicago 9)
- MOST POINTS: 2,856—1,485 games (894 goals, 1,962 assists)
- MOST POINTS, INCLUDING PLAYOFFS: 3,238—2,856 regular season and 382 playoff
- MOST POINTS, ONE SEASON: 215—1985-86, 80-game schedule
- MOST POINTS, ONE SEASON, INCLUDING PLAYOFFS: 255—1984-85; 208 points in 80 regular-season games and 47 points in 18 playoff games
- MOST OVERTIME ASSISTS, CAREER: 15
- MOST GOALS BY A CENTER, CAREER: 894
- MOST GOALS BY A CENTER, ONE SEASON: 92—1981–82, 80-game schedule
- MOST ASSISTS BY A CENTER, CAREER: 1,962
- MOST ASSISTS BY A CENTER, ONE SEASON: 163—1985-86, 80-game schedule
- MOST POINTS BY A CENTER, CAREER: 2,856
- MOST POINTS BY A CENTER, ONE SEASON: 215—1985-86, 80-game schedule
- MOST ASSISTS BY A PLAYER IN HIS FIRST NHL SEASON: 7—Feb. 15, 1980, at Edmonton (Edmonton 8, Washington 2)
- HIGHEST GOALS-PER-GAME AVERAGE, ONE SEASON: 1.18—1983-84, 87 goals in 74 games
- HIGHEST ASSISTS-PER-GAME AVERAGE, CAREER (300 MIN.): 1.321—1,962 assists in 1,485 games
- HIGHEST ASSISTS-PER-GAME AVERAGE, ONE SEASON: 2.04-1985-86, 163 assists in 80 games

- HIGHEST POINTS-PER-GAME AVERAGE, ONE SEASON (AMONG PLAYERS WITH 50-OR-MORE POINTS): 2.77–1983-84, 205 points in 74 games
- MOST 40-OR-MORE GOAL SEASONS: 12 in 20 seasons
- MOST CONSECUTIVE 40-OR-MORE GOAL SEASONS: 12–1979-80 to 1990-91
- MOST 50-OR-MORE GOAL SEASONS: 9 (tied with Mike Bossy)—Wayne in 20 seasons and Bossy in 10 seasons
- MOST 60-OR-MORE GOAL SEASONS: 5 (tied with Mike Bossy)–Wayne in 20 seasons and Bossy in 10 seasons
- MOST CONSECUTIVE 60-OR-MORE GOAL SEASONS: 4–1981-82 to 1984-85
- MOST 100-OR-MORE POINT SEASONS: 15
- MOST CONSECUTIVE 100-OR-MORE POINT SEASONS: 13—1979-80 to 1991-92
- MOST THREE-OR-MORE GOAL GAMES, CAREER: 50—37 three-goal games; nine four-goal games; four five-goal games
- MOST THREE-GOAL GAMES, ONE SEASON: 10 (done twice)—1981-82 (six three-goal games; three four-goal games; one five-goal game) and 1983-84 (six three-goal games, four four-goal games)
- LONGEST CONSECUTIVE ASSIST-SCORING STREAK: 23 games—1990-91, 48 assists
- LONGEST CONSECUTIVE POINT-SCORING STREAK: 51 games—1983-84 (Oct. 5, 1983 to Jan. 28, 1984, 61 goals, 92 assists for 153 points)
- LONGEST CONSECUTIVE POINT-SCORING STREAK FROM START OF SEASON: 51—1983-84; 61 goals, 92 assists for 153 points (Oct. 5, 1983 to Jan. 28, 1984)

Playoff Records (15)

- MOST PLAYOFF GOALS, CAREER: 122
- MOST ASSISTS IN PLAYOFFS, CAREER: 260
- MOST ASSISTS, ONE PLAYOFF YEAR: 31—1988 (19 games)
- MOST ASSISTS IN ONE SERIES (OTHER THAN FINAL): 14—(tied with Rick Middleton) 1985 Conference Finals (six games vs. Chicago)
- MOST ASSISTS IN FINAL SERIES: 10 - 1988 (four games, plus suspended game vs. Boston)
- MOST ASSISTS, ONE PLAYOFF GAME: 6—(tied with Mikko Leinonen) April 9, 1987 at Edmonton (Edmonton 13, Los Angeles 3)
- MOST ASSISTS, ONE PLAYOFF PERIOD: 3—Three assists by one player in one period of a playoff game has been recorded on 70 occasions. Wayne had three assists in one period five times. (Ray Bourque, three times; Toe Blake, Jean Beliveau, Doug Harvey and Bobby Orr, twice.)
- MOST POINTS, CAREER: 382—122 goals and 260 assists
- MOST POINTS, ONE PLAYOFF YEAR: 47—1985 (17 goals and 30 assists in 18 games)
- MOST POINTS IN FINAL SERIES: 13—1988 three goals and 10 assists (four games plus suspended game vs. Boston, three goals)
- MOST POINTS, ONE PLAYOFF PERIOD: 4—(tied with nine other players) April 12, 1987 at Los Angeles, third period, one goal, three assists (Edmonton 6, Los Angeles 3)
- MOST SHORTHANDED GOALS, ONE PLAYOFF YEAR: 3—(tied with five other players) 1983 (two vs. Winnipeg in Division Semi-Finals, won by Edmonton, 3-0; one vs. Calgary in Division Finals, won by Edmonton 4-1)

- MOST SHORT-HANDED GOALS, ONE PLAYOFF GAME: 2—(tied with eight other players) April 6, 1983 at Edmonton (Edmonton 6, Winnipeg 3)
- MOST GAME-WINNING GOALS IN PLAYOFFS, CAREER: 24
- MOST THREE-OR-MORE GOAL GAMES: 10 (eight three-goal games, two four-goal games)

NHL All-Star Game Records (6)

- MOST ALL-STAR GAME GOALS: 13 (in 18 games played)
- MOST ALL-STAR GAME GOALS, ONE GAME: 4—(tied with three players) 1983 Campbell Conference
- MOST ALL-STAR GAME GOALS, ONE PERIOD: 4—1983 Campbell Conference, third period
- MOST ALL-STAR GAME ASSISTS, CAREER: 12—(tied with four players)
- MOST ALL-STAR GAME POINTS, CAREER: 25—(13 goals, 12 assists in 18 games)
- MOST ALL-STAR GAME POINTS, ONE PERIOD: 4—(tied with Mike Gartner and Adam Oates) 1983 Campbell Conference, third period (four goals)

Glossary

assist: A pass to a teammate that results in a goal.

center: One of three players out on the ice whose primary responsibility is to score. These players are called forwards. The forward in the middle is the *center*. The other two forwards are the *left wing* and *right wing*.

center ice: The neutral zone between the two blue lines.

check: The use of one's body or stick to take the puck away from an opponent or to block or hit the opponent so that he or she loses control of the puck.

defensemen: Players who help the goaltender protect their team's goal. A team has two defensemen out on the ice at a time.

hat trick: The scoring of three or more goals by the same person in one game.

line: A set of three forwards—center, right wing, and left wing—that normally plays together.

points: Credits given to a player for scoring a goal or assisting on one. A player gets one point for a goal and one point for an assist.

power play: The offense used when one's team has more players on the ice because the other team has one or more players in the penalty box.

winger: A forward who plays on the left or right side.

zone: A team's zone is the area between that team's goal and the nearest blue line.

Index

Acknowledgments

Photographs are reproduced with permission of: © John Giamundo/
Bruce Bennett Studios, p. 1; AP/Wide World Photos, pp. 2, 6, 55;
© Bruce Bennett/Bruce Bennett Studios, pp. 10, 13, 50, 53, 58;
Brantford Expositor, pp. 15, 17, 20; Westfile Archive, pp. 24, 46;
Westfile/Bob Mummery, p. 29; Bill McKeown, p. 32; Westfile/Bill
McKeown, pp. 38, 43.

Front cover photograph by © Bruce Bennett/Bruce Bennett Studios.
Back cover photograph by © Scott Levy/Bruce Bennett Studios.